Grace

Dorethie Willing

Grace

Grace
ISBN 978 1 76109 232 9
Copyright © Mark Willing 2021

First published 2021 by
Ginninderra Press
PO Box 3461 Port Adelaide 5015
www.ginninderrapress.com.au

Contents

Preface	7
Grandmother, My Grandmother	9
In My Imagination	10
My Father	11
Train Travels	13
The Painting	14
Waiting For Rain	15
The Smallest Flower	16
Silent Tribute	17
The Early Dark	18
Nostalgia	19
Old Photographs	20
Beginnings and Endings	21
Friend	22
A Double Life	23
A Tribute	25
Fantasy	26
Chance Encounter	27
Interlude	28
The Busker	29
Sky Wonders	30
On Reflection	31
My Memory Cupboard	32
A Million Books	33
Differences	34
Night Fright	35
Night Vigil	36
Roaring Into Life	37
Street Walk	38

The Love of Travelling	40
The Christmas Box	41
Quiet Celebration	42
Thirteen	43
Déjà vu	44
This Here and Now	45
The Journey	46
The Lollipop Man	47
My Child Within	48
Missing In Action	49
The Earth Mourns	50
Maranoa	51
Instant Music	52
Morning at Albert Park	54
Grace	55

Preface

These are some of the poems written by Doretha (Dorethie) Willing, who only recently passed away at the age of 101. Dorethie was born and raised in the suburbs of Adelaide but moved to Melbourne just after World War II. A classically trained soprano, Dorethie spent much of her life singing in various choirs including the Melbourne Philharmonic, Camberwell Chorale and numerous church choirs. Music had always been her life's passion. However, when she was in her seventies, Dorethie joined a writing group at U3A in Mont Albert and developed a love of literature, especially poetry. She later became convener of the Blackburn Writers' Group and was an active participant up until her mid-nineties, when poor health required that she move into an aged care facility. At ninety-eight years of age, Dorethie started the Lynden Aged Care Writers' Group which met monthly until just before her one hundredth birthday.

These are the poems of one who worked hard all her life and had to make ends meet. Dorethie enjoyed her independent life in retirement and wrote many of her poems on the front veranda of her apartment, overlooking a serene garden. They are poems of introspection, sadness, loneliness and yet there is a sense of pride in all she has achieved which has led her to this place of meditation. The poems possess a bitter-sweet tone borne from her joys and hardships.

Dorethie's poems reflect experiences from her childhood as well as later life living alone, but with a sense of peace drawn from her strong Christian faith. There is a poignant melancholy present in many of her experiences and reflections.

Dorethie relates everyday scenes incorporating moods that switch between loneliness, regret and then sheer joy of independence. A trip to a local nursery is a joyous event but simultaneously there is a backdrop of an otherwise dismal day. As a young child, she and her mother are watching a train with young men jauntily marching to board it. But in the mind of the young girl, why are they marching?

I would like to thank Ginninderra Press for this opportunity to bring Dorethie Willing's poetry to a wider audience. This book will certainly provide family and friends with a memento they can hold onto for a long time.

Mark Willing

Grandmother, My Grandmother

Again I recall the vision you left me
your strength of purpose
against adversity
the Great Depression
the pain of poverty
I admired, respected you.

Those childhood memories
your welcoming smile
those after-school visits
with ginger cake and lemonade
beneath your spreading garden trees.

Black astrakhan hat and gloves
the long walk to our house
your quick step on the porch
little gifts for all.

Perhaps some little twig
from that family tree
still lives in me
and in my children
and still the vision to nourish
that it may bloom and flourish.

In My Imagination

I travel to faraway places
revisiting tender moments
even trespassing on yesterday's memories.

High in a New York apartment
my Parisian neighbour
sends me tiny silk flowers
hot colours and a latte.

A whirlwind rises from the page of my book
and fills the house with extraordinary places.
I go out into the garden and peace returns.
I can run like the wind through the park
along the river bank to the high street
avoiding a straggle of shoppers
throw myself on the park bench
under the great oak and listen.

Revisit the old schoolhouse
in Canadian country where corn grows high
sit in the sun in the window
with company and coffee
recalling more with my imagination.

My Father

In the early twenties, horse-drawn vehicles were the mode of transport. Carts and vans, even public transport, were in the stage of being developed. It was a common sight to see troughs and tether posts where horses were left by their owners, sometimes for hours while shopping and other business was done. We attended a large church where the churchyard was equipped with troughs along each fence and on Sunday mornings the buggies of all shapes and sizes and their horses were lined up and it was a sea of black. These were the Sunday vehicles and they were immaculate.

My parents owned a large black buggy with back-to-back seating. We three children sat at the back, our parents in front. In winter, the hood was raised and we were covered with a water-proof, fur-lined rug. We owned two horses, Creamy and Bronco, and it was Bronco who was used at weekends. They were kept in the third allotment where the stables were situated. Bronco was black and shiny and Creamy was the work horse. They were well fed and groomed and I remember my dad mixing their bran and pollard each morning in winter with warm water. The stables were off limits for us but the chicken coop was nearby and we were allowed to collect the eggs under supervision.

I remember on one occasion we had planned a family picnic at Glenelg Beach. At that time, the steam train travelled along Jetty Road as the trams do today. Bronco was upset by the whistle and the sound of the engine and refused to move. We had just crossed the train line but it was still too close for comfort. As the train came closer, Dad jumped down and tried to lead Bronco away but he refused to budge. We were all very afraid when he finally reared up and pulled away to safety. It was a scary experience for us all, even the horse. Not long after, my dad bought our first car.

Train Travels

I feel the chill of Mt Lofty station
clutching my mother's hand.
I am a child, stepping into the morning mist.
On the crowded platform
we watch solemnly
as the troops pass by
muffled sound of army boots
the Forty-Third Battalion
marching to catch the train
marching to war.

The Painting

The lake is placid
overhung by willows
white sails of two small boats
the only sign of life.
I see more
of the artist's brush strokes
where grasses grow low.
Mountains in the background
rise from the far bank.
I feel more
the life of the painter
her gift to me
as she flees with her children
to safety
shedding family
familiar sights and sounds
fashion and customs
for unknown places.
I treasure all I have of her
whispers from a dark past
wish the peace of the lake for her
on her journey.

Waiting For Rain

From the shadowy porch
worn stone steps
lead down to open spaces
unbroken distance

The country simmers in quiet heat
a bee searches for a flower
an old bridge spans its dry creek bed
a few sheep nibble tufts of green
two rosellas swoop across our path
toward the gums along the creek

Along the path
scraggy evergreens struggle
from a dying hedge
dust flares from the paddocks
he stoops to crumble a handful of earth
pats the white bole of a towering gum
walks on where clusters shrivel on the vines

A trail of ants braves the burning path
going somewhere.

The Smallest Flower

It grows beneath the garden's mantle
of flowering shrub and towering tree
with head bowed low
it hides its hue
to live unnoticed
and alone

It does not seek a higher place
in profusion or on display
but modestly remains
for those who chance upon
the smallest flower
the subtle colour of its name –
violet.

Silent Tribute

Someone has been here today
remembering
flowers by the roadside
tied to a pole
leaving the message
he was loved.

No screaming sirens
searching lights
no cries of pain
or tears
just the stillness
and remembrance.

The Early Dark

The dark creeps in
amid the calm and drift of dusk
to snatch the light
to steal the day.

Too soon
street lights burn
steps quicken
on dark pavements.

Eager tyres squish along
beneath processions of light
where houses
lamp lit
string out like pearls
come alive in the dual night.

Nostalgia

Remembering World War II, when I followed my husband to his camp in Strathalbyn. Our child was six weeks old and life was in turmoil for many people.

I passed a rustic bridge
in bright revealing sunlight
and suddenly remembered other days
a dusty road
another bridge
when war was raging
and we walked on unfamiliar paths.

The memory wakened loneliness
and strange nostalgia gripped me
tempted me to live again
those days of dislocation.

And suddenly, here and now
the same nostalgia claims me
that other place
the rustic bridge
as in a dream
the scene returns

To haunt me once again.

Old Photographs

Sepia
black and white
unknown faces
look out from foreign backgrounds
sons once loved
nurtured
grown into manhood
slouch hat   stripes
lost in time
in memory.

Beginnings and Endings

A patch of blue within a darkening sky
a tiny patch amid the clouds
I cling to its colour
knowing it will vanish.

I touch the first flower
velvet magnolia
inhale its perfume
it will fade and fall
leave no trace.

The space my parents used to fill
their caring hands
that made me what I am
brought me to this day.
I never dreamed that they would be no more
leaving me alone.

Each day is bright with promise
I make my plans to live it well
but all is change –
a reaping and replanting.

Friend

I see the ivy-covered wall
the silver birch where once we sheltered
her flower pots no longer in bloom
the hose coiled nearby

The vacant driveway
closed garage
her favourite roses
sometimes picked for me
now pruned and bare

I long to see the blinds raised high
feel that she is there
but she no longer knows or cares

And when the bells of St Dominics
resound with clanging echoes
she can no longer hear them
for she is far away
in solitude

She cannot now recall those days
or ivy-covered wall
or silver birch, or me.

A Double Life

She minces along
cars slow, horns blow
people turn and stare
her stilettos tap
her dress swirls
as Marilyn passes by.

A wave, a smile
she flaunts to be noticed
confident
head high
to walk like a queen.

Soft blonde hair
frames her fragile face
red lips pout
whisper and croon
her Marilyn songs.

Often outrageous
to shock or distract
ignores her critics
to follow her trend
of low-cut, transparent
skirts split revealing
sequins, satin
velvet and pearls

A life of pretence
she drifts in a dream
embraces the image
no longer real
flits like a butterfly
colourful, free

But loneliness haunts
her solitary hours
those sleepless nights
realities of queens.

A Tribute

He travelled far
a strangely silent man.
Unhurried, uninvited
knowing his own time
to find his place
where friendships start
grow and remain.

Awakened
thought became action in him
to feel
explore
reach out

Became a voice of reason
seeker of dreams
constant in crisis
calm in despair

Knew his worth
made his mark

Time intervened
he walked in shadow
faced a setting sun.

Through tears and rain
I watched the casket
flower-strewn but shaded
move along the busy road
out of sight.

Fantasy

Sand, sea and sky
a waiting place

Deserted still
where gulls fly high
and tireless ripples lap and flow

Yet in the dunes
the small rowboat
unmanned, expectantly
waits

It waits in vain
no calloused hands
to lift it to the sea
cast it adrift to ride the waves
to cross the blue eternity

It waits
and in my dream
sand, sea and sky
deserted, still.

Chance Encounter

She stands at the bus stop
a cold wind lifts her thin jacket
teases grey hair
she is alone

The handbag hangs from her wrist
at her feet the laden basket
anxious eyes study the timetable
search the horizon

He ambles along
pauses at the stop
scruffy jacket, worn jeans
grubby runners
he paces
then leans
stubs out the cigarette

Dull eyes focus on grey hair
and then the handbag

The bus slows
he picks up the basket
helps her aboard
she smiles

He slumps into a seat
and sleeps.

Interlude

A dismal day
no plans
then inspiration
a trip to the Acorn Nursery.

A kindly passer-by
directs me to a parking space
right next to the entrance
where a maze of hanging baskets
islands of colour
massed plants in flower
greets me.

Now to the herb garden
parsley, thyme, coriander
a pansy pot
time to breathe in the displays.

I explore the gift shop
a latte at the café
my favourite cherry pie
two small flowers adorn my plate.

I encounter the kindly passer-by
and thank him
a pleasant interlude
on such a dismal day.

The Busker

Gnarled fingers grasp the tarnished sax
its old tune mellow, haunting
unheeded by passers-by
he plays on
his shabby hat placed to beg.

Perched high upon its stool
his grey poodle crouches low
matted coat, watery eyes
it watches him
and waits.

The small boy tugs her hand
they pause
to drop a coin
drowned out by pounding feet
without a glance.

Sky Wonders

The first blush of dawn
skies kaleidoscopic
fingers of light stretch and search
a sleeping world

Wind sweeps clouds away
from the blue expanse
a canopy
above mountain peaks
tide wash
and city sprawl

The sun, suspended high
ever-present, even in storms
sometimes a mere promise
like a rainbow
or the end of day

A western glow
as shadows lengthen
until the sun drops
like a gold coin
into the pocket of night

Twilight
starry skies
another journey
unheralded
begins.

On Reflection

Mirrored in soft lamplight
the perfume bottle gleams
sometimes I see
remember the gift
and feel a presence in the room

They crowd around
these people in my past
but I so often visit
with unseeing eyes
and pass them by
unnoticed

My mother's face
now framed in silver
the flowery jug and basin
precious in my childhood home
the perfume bottle
clinging memories
of her dying

The lace-trimmed photo on the wall
two small faces smiling
and I was there

so long ago
        oh how we danced on the night we were wed
that haunting tune of the jewellery box
and I can barely touch
recall
relive
these moments from my past.

My Memory Cupboard

I look across the room and through the glass window of my china cupboard. I see a collection of pieces that I treasure.
The little cup and saucer inscribed in German and gold lettering, 'Das Lieben Kind'.
The silver tea service presented to my grandfather in 1905. Just fifty-two when he died. I was his first grandchild.
My funny face egg cup I used as a child.
Fine china teacups, a gift from a dear neighbour. 'Think of me when you use this.' I do.
The roses cup from my school friend Jean, when we were fourteen.
The piece of blue Limoges, a gift from the registrar of a university in Canada.
The very large cup and saucer, inscribed in German 'Hausherrn', from my grandmother's collection.
When I take the time to look, I see again the people I have known and loved through the window of my china cabinet.

A Million Books

We clatter up the well-worn stairs
tread the squeaky boards
bespectacled behind his ancient desk
his eyes alert
he answers and directs.

This is the house of a million books
a collector's dream
reader's paradise
from floor to ceiling shelves extend
along the dusty aisles.

Ladders run along their rails
attendants clamber on request
posters decorate and depict
and along the walls the shabby desks
where students gather, search and read.

The busy silence shuffles
tiptoes on the bare-board floor
flick of pages
whispered findings
to question or reply.

Our quest completed
satisfied
we leave this shadowy place
vowing to return
when next the search begins.

Differences

I see what she sees
yet differently
restless she sighs and smiles
and wanders on
while I linger captivated.

I hear her music
those same notes play another tune:
for her a meadow dance
along the keyboard
for me a performance
in a great hall.

We share our passion
shady peripheries
so much more beautiful in her mind
for me the struggle of the eldest.

We are sisters
ties exist
make us family
but ideas and tastes force us apart
to challenge and confuse
even suffer.

Night Fright

Sleep-starved eyes
search the blackness
yesterday's doubts
become shadowy giants
ghostly
and menacing.

Imaginary outcomes
now mountains of misery
thoughts race with
unwanted images
heart beats with
untold fear.

Daylight.
The torment fades.
Sleep claims it.

Night Vigil

A strange sound punctuates the silence
disturbs my sleep
baffles
annoys

Lured to explore
along the path
snails crunch underfoot
it's just me and the moon
at this late hour

Ghostly shadows
a fickle breeze
to rouse the trees
the midnight cat
weaves about my feet
a possum treads along the fence

Moonlight dapples my path
the sound fades
I retrace my steps
hear it more clearly
now from above

High on the swaying cable
in bright moonlight
the white owl drones.

Roaring Into Life

In the carpark
behind Safeway
she sits cross-legged
on the kerb

Crumpled T-shirt
faded jeans
barefoot
her life in her backpack
she smokes a cigarette
reads a tattered paperback
and waits

The old van chugs to a stop
she clambers in
it shudders
roars into life
and drives away.

Street Walk

A suburb away
another world
same trams glide along the High Street
cars align beneath broad plane trees
shoppers walk the pavements

But fashions are trendy
expensive
small shops crowd along the strip
dark interiors
strange window displays

Quaint hole-in-the-wall spaces
along the arcade
painted in bright colours
racks of jewellery
bric-a-brac

Shopping strips stretch in both directions
exhibitions of art
photography
antique galleries
historic buildings well-preserved

At the rear a park brings relief
birds play at the water feature
the young man strums a guitar
a French coffee shop offers its gallery
photography of Tour de France

Racks of pre-loved garments
pressed together
strollers loiter around cluttered windows
life at a different pace
in another place

a suburb away.

The Love of Travelling

In my own space and time
I move from the known to the unknown
travel to distant horizons
over land and sea

Where snow-clad mountains tower
great rivers flow
cities hum with vitality
colourful villages and simple lifestyles
exist and thrive.

The journeys are endless
effortless, inexpensive
readily available
from my armchair.

The Christmas Box

December comes
you emerge from your darkness
to share your contents
celebrate another year.

Tinsel, silver stars
the wreath for the door
collection of ornaments
to adorn the tree.

The angel in white velvet gown
gold stars in her hair
a reindeer carved from pine
the bird of paradise
so bright with colour
and balls of shimmering glass
reflecting the glow of the lights

Each hung with care
like memories
all having their time and space
to disappear again
at year's end.

Quiet Celebration

Another year
a simple tribute
the rose withers
petals fall
she smiles out from her silver frame

Her eyes meet mine
I feel her presence
see her hair
the string of pearls
her wedding ring

Years have passed
pain dimmed her eyes
lonely days
remembering her

Her garden
cosmos growing tall
violets low beneath the hedge
books
her songs and family fun

I know them all
these memories strong
of things she taught
all she hoped I would be.

Thirteen

She remembers thirteen
that in-between year
so many questions
about so many things
lectured
advised
she listens

Trapped in school uniform
hair tight in braids
feet firm in lace-ups
gawky
unsure
obsessed with the pain
of her puerile state

She pouts as she loiters
in corners of fashion stores
searching for styles
too in-mode for her age
the mirrors reflect
a pale ambition

Anxious to please
longing to be praised
brash – but she crumples
dissolves into tears
test-fights authority

Cruel teenage years.

Déjà vu

Strange familiarity
a feeling I've been here before
but only tangled memories now persist.

I look around me
search for that elusive proof
where ancient buildings now restored
stand proud.

This strange nostalgia grips me
and I shiver
longing to clarify its mystery
compelled by absurd desire
to travel back to where I began.

And then I see her.
A sense of the familiar
hovers, taunts me
until still pondering
she walks away.

This Here and Now

No need to wonder
where the roads not travelled lead
what wonders lie in other lands
beyond our reach.

No need to envy others who succeed
on paths we did not choose
or yearn for who we might have been
if time had let our talents be

Or mourn forever
faces once held dear.
These loosened steps along the way
have led us to our now and here.

The Journey

Earth turns
seasons flow
gather the seeds of the past
provide for them a resurrection soil.

Fall in love with loving
but keep the memories
of those you met along the way
recalling pleasures of the past.

Wrestle with pain and chaos
within yourself and the world
join the celebration of life
dancing with angels and clowns.

Feel acceptance and rejection
but leave them as you move along
beyond their influence.
Live with positivity and hope.

And may the God of peace and joy
who makes all things new
embrace you as a partner
in this world and the next.

The Lollipop Man

Who dares to move across
his sacred space
without consent?
He rules his small selected place
and we obey.

The children cluster at the curb
prepare to brave the bustling road
he steps across
stands on guard
his eyes shout volumes
and we wait.

He wears the uniform with pride
and trusting children
smile and chat.
At his command
a human tide
stops traffic with a lollipop.

My Child Within

Touch sometimes blurs
as I encounter
my child within.

Those long-forgotten ways
whisperings from the past
through some mysterious half-light
she emerges.

Real or imagined
she now exists
retains her powers
shares unfinished business
with familiar reminders

Pink floral pinafore
long socks with ankle straps
wide straw hat
shading long, blonde hair
childish voice singing
dancing feet springing
happily pushing her small wicker pram.

Wistfully watching her finite world
boisterously voicing certainty or fear
this child awakens a shadowy past
a hand returns to caress again

And I embrace
my child within.

Missing In Action

Just one day in each year
I think of you
when flags fly at half mast
while bands play
and families, some in uniform, march
I think of you.

So young
so well-prepared
you wore the Blue with pride
the Flight Lieutenant's cap
to share the danger
with your crew of five.

So many years have passed
since we were twenty-one
when into danger unafraid
where bullets struck
planes dived to bomb
your world in flames
you died.

Your mother wore three silver stars
one for each son who served
but only two came home from war
her youngest lost on foreign soil
or in the ocean far away.

The bugler plays the Last Post.
Those who remember bow their heads
and I recall those final words
Missing In Action.

The Earth Mourns

We do not hear its groans
or feel its pain.
Overpopulated
it suffers the weight
of the uncaring.

Rivers polluted
forests destroyed
replaced by sprawling cities
and their lavish lives.

It yields treasure
deposits, gold and silver
metals, coal and oil
delving leaves its surface barren.

War and conflict
areas laid waste
littered shorelines
life threatened.

Fire and flood disrupt
destroy
soil infertile
habitats disappear.

Seasons roll on.
The earth mourns.

Maranoa

Hidden in suburbia
silent as a secret
which when found
excites, enraptures

Stonework pillars
heritage gates
entrance to a world
of a forgotten past

Unique assemblage
of native flora
treasured reflection
of a century of care

Beneath the scented gum
majestic in its skyward reach
I ask to leave the remnants of my life
to sink in its soil

disappear.

Instant Music

My father was a great musician. He could produce such masterpieces as the Zampa and Poet and Peasant Overtures, the Hallelujah Chorus, even a Dvorak Humoresque at the flick of a switch and some good, even pedalling.

I was five years old when the large, dark player piano arrived at our house. Its name above the keyboard read Brunswick and it came from America. It was a wonder to us as children to see and hear our father produce such beautiful music. The notes danced along as if magic fingers were touching them. There were long boxes stacked at the side and rolls of paper with small holes were taken out, attached, then switched on. Only adults could pedal as our legs were too short.

There was Peter Rabbit and nursery rhymes with pictures, children's songs and hymns and we marched to the sounds of Washington Post, The American Patrol and Stars and Stripes. We loved the sad songs too. 'Play a sad song, Dad' and he would choose The End of a Perfect Day, Ave Maria and our favourite, Ora Pro Nobis.

Out in the dark and dreary street
Out in the cold and driving sleet
Into the church the folk had gone
Leaving the orphan child alone

Tattered and so forlorn was she
They crossed themselves as they passed
To see so frail a child in grievous plight
On such a relentless stormy night.

That was a real tear-jerker and we loved it.

In later years, the piano remained a great source of entertainment. We accumulated a large collection of rolls. Our friends would gather around to sing and dance, choosing their favourite music. During the war, many homesick American Army boys enjoyed our hospitality and my sisters and I still have memories of the friends we made.

The piano was tuned and polished and there were rules about who played it and when. It was a fine instrument enjoyed by all our family and friends over many years. When we were married, left home and our father had died, the piano was donated to a charity.

I personally took up piano lessons when I was six. My teacher was a hard task master. I can recall playing at a recital in the Town Hall with my fingers taped after the sharp taps from the stick which always resided on his piano ledge. Apparently I never inherited my father's finesse.

Morning at Albert Park

Across the plantation
from the walled convent
the silence now broken
by the never-ending traffic
the blue-stone wall extends into the distance
a jogger pounds the esplanade.

The lonely seat beckons
in the sun's warmth.
I gaze out over the bay
a smoky grey ocean
meets the skyline
to merge.

The *Spirit of Tasmania* on a glassy sea
two labradors romp and roll
gulls whirl and call
land at my feet
and wait expectantly.

At the water's edge
waves ripple to meet
a deserted shoreline
shells and seaweed aqua clear
under the wavering prism of the current.
I trudge back
sinking into the gorgeous coarse sand.

All this so far
and yet so near
to a bustling city.
Here is peace.

Grace

Living is a dailiness
with its bread of survival.
I have known a wine
rich and flowing
on days bright with promise
and opportunity.

But now clouds gather
days are long
steps slow
the bread still offered
but the wine no longer flows.

But good intentions flourish
and memories
reminders of those days.
The flowers still bloom.
Peaceful days follow nights
offer small joys.

And this is grace.

www.ingramcontent.com/pod-product-compliance
Lightning Source LLC
Chambersburg PA
CBHW062204100526
44589CB00014B/1943